Living with Wolves

Wolves

Jim and Jamie Dutcher

With Helen Cherullo and James Manfull

The Mountaineers Books
SEATTLE

dedicated to the sawtooth pack

Thank you for trusting us and changing our lives.

Your willingness to allow us into your family

has paved the way for your story and the story of all wolves.

You will always be in our hearts as we fight for wild wolves

and for the wilderness needed to let your spirits run free.

CONTENTS

FOREWORD

By William H. Meadows
President of The Wilderness Society

"You can't just let nature run wild," said Alaska Governor Walter Hickel in the 1990s when he was trying to build support for hunting wolves from airplanes.

Today, more and more wolves are running wild, a great achievement, especially at a time when the natural world is under such broad attack. Some of the credit certainly goes to Jamie and Jim Dutcher, whose creativity and dedication has done so much to educate the public about wolves. Long-held attitudes about a species can be tougher to eliminate than the species itself, but the Dutchers' books and films have helped puncture some of the myths about wolves.

Changing attitudes is one part of the battle to restore wolves to their natural role. Another is making sure they have a home. For wolves, there is no home like wilderness. The places where they have survived, such as the Greater Yellowstone Ecosystem and Alaska, provide wildness where wolves can find food, shelter, and solitude.

Because wolves have received such bad press for so long, few people realize the benefits that a healthy wolf population can provide. Scientists have documented important changes at Yellowstone since the wolf was restored there in 1995. Because wolves feed on elk, herds no longer congregate along streams and rivers, where they were simply too vulnerable to attack. The result has been a comeback by cottonwood, willows, and other riverbank trees that elk had overgrazed. Once these trees became healthy, migratory birds returned. The shade created by the trees also cools the water, making it habitable for trout again—and the trout provide protein for grizzlies. Low-hanging willow branches offer food for beavers, which by 1996 had disappeared from Yellowstone. Their dams are now creating marshland that is home to otters and mink.

These are just some of the most obvious changes in the Yellowstone ecosystem. As a keystone species at the top of the food chain, the wolf plays a central role. Once this species is removed, as it was when land managers thought the slaughter of wolves was sound public policy, the ecosystem falls out of balance.

So what can we do to make sure that we—and the generations that inherit our natural legacy—have balanced, functioning natural systems? One fundamental and critical goal is to save wilderness. Saving irreplaceable land has been The Wilderness Society's mission since its creation in 1935. Many of the wild places left in the United States already belong to the American people. ▷

They are found in our national parks, national forests, national wildlife refuges, and the Western land overseen by the U.S. Bureau of Land Management. Of these 626 million acres, 106 million have been judged sufficiently pristine to be included in the National Wilderness Preservation System. Now protected by law, this wilderness haven, only 5 percent of our nation's land, is free from the sounds, development, and intrusions of man.

These special places are much more than campsites and hiking destinations. They provide the cleanest drinking water available. They scrub our air. They serve as natural laboratories where researchers are discovering tomorrow's medicines. Because of their appeal, they serve as anchors for the fast-growing tourism and recreation industry.

For wildlife, it does not get any better than wilderness. The great Western herds, migratory birds, and predators such as the grizzly and wolf have a chance to survive if we can protect enough wilderness to sustain them. This reality is clear not only in the Northern Rockies but in northwestern Wisconsin, northern Minnesota, Michigan's Isle Royale National Park, the forests of Maine, southeastern Arizona, and in the hardwood forests and coastal swamps of North Carolina's Alligator River National Wildlife Refuge, where the red wolf was successfully reintroduced.

The Dutchers understand this need for wild land as well as anyone. They are spirited conservationists who champion the wilderness cause, at a time when we need champions more than ever. Wilderness is threatened by oil and

gas drilling, logging, mining, out-of-control off-road vehicle use, and more. We are heartened that so many grassroots groups are taking action to safeguard wild places near and dear to them by persuading Congress to add them to the Wilderness System. Their success will help make it possible to carry on Jim and Jamie's dream of wild wolves in wild places.

The howl of the wolf has long been considered "the call of the wild." It was nearly silenced in the continental United States. All of us who cherish the natural world are indebted to the Dutchers for their extraordinary work in reversing the wolf's fortunes. Anyone who reads this fascinating book will understand the size of that debt.

PREFACE: FOUR PERCEPTIONS OF WOLVES

By Jim and Jamie Dutcher

In our many years of studying wolves, we found that people have four different perceptions of wolves that often exist side by side.

The first of these perceptions is what we call the *wolf of our nightmares*. This is the beast of ancient fears, the concept of the wolf that the Europeans brought with them to the New World. This savage creature lingers today in the minds of many ranchers and hunters: a bloodthirsty killer of livestock, big-game animals, and even human beings. Sadly, this view holds fast despite mountains of evidence to the contrary.

The second perception we often see is the carefully monitored *wolf of science*—the wolf pursued and studied by biologists. This wolf is often depicted through data—statistics of breeding, predation, physiology, and travel. Although this view does acknowledge the wolf's intelligence, it often turns a blind eye to the wolf's individuality, to its devotion to its family, and to anything that hints at its capacity for emotion.

On the opposite end of the spectrum is the third perception—what we call the *spirit wolf*. This creature, honored in the culture of many Native American tribes, has been borrowed and often distorted by modern wolf advocates. This wolf is an animal of great wisdom to be revered as a spiritual guide. Although this view holds the wolf in great esteem, it often does so at the expense of accurate scientific knowledge about the animal.

Finally, there is the wolf that we have come to know—the *social wolf*. In our years of living with and observing these animals, we learned to see them as individuals, each with its own distinct personality. Yet they were intensely social creatures, extremely devoted to their pack—their family. Time and time again, we saw the great affection and care they demonstrate for one another and concluded that they are capable of not only emotion but also real compassion. This is the view of the wolf that we want to share—a wolf that is neither demon nor deity nor biological robot. It is an intelligent and highly sensitive animal that can be at once both individualistic and social. It is an animal that cares for its sick, protects its family, and desperately needs to be part of something bigger than itself—the pack.

ACKNOWLEDGMENTS

Jim and Jamie wish to offer their appreciation to the following people:

To Garrick Dutcher and James Manfull, who contributed so much hard work and dedication to our films and books and who shared our love of wolves. We would also like to thank all the members of our crew from wolf camp—especially Keith Marshall.

For their support and constant encouragement, Sherri Baker, Alan and Melinda Blinken, Kathleen Brown, Dave Dickie, Jim and Lucia Gilliland, Jed Gray, Johann Guschelbauer, Bill Innes, Dennis Kane, Senator John Kerry and Teresa Heinz Kerry, the Idaho Department of Fish and Game, Glenn Janss, Kathy McCormack, Bill Meadows and The Wilderness Society, William S. Merwin, the Nez Perce tribe, Karin Rundquist, Pam Simpson, Van Gordon Sauter, the United States Forest Service, Diana and Mallory Walker, Jan Wygle, and Zuri.

We would like to thank our friend, Norma Douglas, who believed in our story and supported us in making this book happen, including finding our extraordinary publisher, Helen Cherullo. We would also like to honor the memory of Marshall Douglas, who sat with us and his daughter and who patiently shared so many years of talk about books, film, and, of course, wolves.

INTRODUCTION: A JOURNEY THROUGH MEMORY

By James Manfull

And when, on the still cold nights, he pointed his nose at a star and howled long and wolf-like, it was his ancestors, dead and dust, pointing nose at star and howling down through the centuries and through him.

—Jack London, *The Call of the Wild*

It wasn't supposed to turn out like this. When filmmaker Jim Dutcher made his first steps toward a project about the North American gray wolf, he had imagined that this charismatic animal would be just another subject in a lifetime of wildlife filmmaking. Even as the project unfolded, Jim and his wife, Jamie, looked forward to future work documenting other creatures and ecosystems of North America and beyond.

But something changed. One film became two. The original two-year project grew to four years, then six. A fascination with wolves became an obsession and, finally, a life calling that has only grown stronger with the passing decades. It has drawn the Dutchers far from their familiar role of filmmakers into the center of the fierce controversy over wolf management and land use in the American West.

Most important, their ongoing relationship with this animal has brought forth two Emmy-winning films. Jim's project, *Wolf: Return of a Legend,* aired on ABC's *World of Discovery* in 1993. That same year, Jamie joined him to make *Wolves at Our Door* for the Discovery Channel, airing in 1997. These two programs shed much-needed light on the most mythologized, misunderstood, and persecuted predator on the North American continent.

Wolves by nature are wary and elusive creatures. They are extremely difficult to see in the wild, let alone film. People—even those with good intentions—can pose a threat to the animal's welfare if the wolf loses its natural fear of humans. Jim wanted to film wolves up close in a relaxed and untroubled state, and the only way to do that was to form a pack of wolves that would be completely comfortable in the presence of humans. In preparation for realizing this vision, in 1990 Jim and his team designed an enclosure, with acres of alpine meadows, streams, and forest on the edge of wilderness in Idaho's Sawtooth Mountains, a home where the wolves could have a natural habitat with abundant space to roam.

Next, Jim acquired two adult wolves from wolf rescue centers. After establishing the adults, he introduced four pups, born to other captive wolves, and in later years he added two more small litters. He and his crew gave American Indian names to identify each wolf but made no attempt to teach

the wolves their names or to initiate behavior or interaction. Everything was conducted on the wolves' terms.

Over the course of the following years, the wolves matured, established a hierarchy, and even mated and produced offspring. The Dutchers lived in a tented camp within the wolves' territory—a constant but unobtrusive presence—documenting, recording, and photographing life inside the pack.

The Dutchers' approach—one of social partnership with the animals—has garnered discussion, debate, criticism, and, most often, appreciation and encouragement. Jim's camera work and Jamie's sound recording have created a more intimate portrayal of wolves than ever could have been achieved through impassive observation. As a result, audiences have become acquainted with an animal that, in addition to being a successful predator, is curious, playful, individualistic, and resolutely devoted to family. The Dutchers' films, books, and speaking engagements continue to command large and diverse audiences eager to know more about the wolf pack they have come to cherish.

Today, a decidedly chilly one in late October, the Dutchers, along with Jim's thirty-three-year-old son, Garrick, are setting out to satisfy that need, continuing to share stories and experiences gathered during six years of living with wolves. They are returning to the site of their long-dismantled wolf camp to shoot new footage for a two-hour Discovery Channel special. Their destination lies in an area called the Sawtooth Wilderness, about an hour and a half northwest of their home in Ketchum, Idaho.

Jim pilots the four-wheel drive, loaded with camera gear, food, and warm clothes, up Highway 75, over breathtaking Galena Summit, and down into the valley along the headwaters of the Salmon River. At the tiny village of Stanley, they cut southwest onto a narrow jeep track toward the rocky spires of the Sawtooth Mountains. At the base of Williams Peak, they reach their destination: a bright meadow dotted with stands of willow, aspen, and spruce, bordered by an icy stream. Years ago, this was wolf camp.

It is a moody sort of day—uncommon for this time of year. Cascades of mist spill over the saddle of Williams Peak and into the forest of lodgepole pine. But the sky is clearing. Winter is not far away, though it looks as if it will hold off for today. Jim steps from the vehicle and, along with Garrick and Jamie, begins to set up the camera and audio gear. Together they trek up the gentle slope.

Six feet tall and slender, clad in Levi's and a wide-brim hat, Jim Dutcher has the appearance and gait of an Idaho rancher. His movements are fluid and purposeful, his steps careful over the delicate terrain. Surprisingly, he spent most of his young life in Florida, coming out west only on rare occasions. When he was five years old, his father bought him a Brownie Hawkeye camera and a crude underwater housing, feeding a fascination with documenting the natural world that eventually became a career. Dutcher's first subjects were the coral reefs and marine life in Florida and the Caribbean. Seeing him now in this

western wilderness setting, however, it is difficult to imagine him anywhere else. He even admits to sometimes feeling reluctant about his new role as wolf advocate—the meetings, the lectures, the television interviews. It is clear that this is where he belongs, out on a mountain slope, beneath a shimmering canopy of aspens and the open Idaho sky.

Garrick, Jim's son, takes over the role of cameraperson today, since his father and Jamie are the subjects. He is shooting footage for a scene they're calling "Remembering the Past." No acting is required.

The Dutchers have not had reason to set foot here for many years. Their Forest Service permit to use this land expired in 1996, and the wolves were moved to a similar situation that Jim designed for them on the reservation of the Nez Perce tribe, nine hours to the north. At the old site, seasons of frost, thaw, and growth have erased all traces of humans and wolves, as the Dutcher's intended. This is, quite literally, a journey through memory.

As Garrick films, Jim Dutcher scans the landscape, remembering. When he speaks, his voice is like his movements: careful, quiet, and measured. "It's strange, seeing this place as it is now," he says. "The way it used to be is burned onto my mind."

Through his eyes, the old camp begins to materialize. In the center of the meadow on an eight-foot-high platform stood the Mongolian-style yurt that served as kitchen, eating area, workshop, and center of camp life. Beside it was the canvas wall tent where the Dutchers slept. By the forest's edge stood the shower tent, where a bag of solar-heated creek water provided a touch of comfort and civility.

Summers at wolf camp were idyllic times for the Dutchers, when the sky was an endless blue and daylight lingered long into the evening. But winter was the wolves' time. Their cold-weather coats seemed to almost double their size and made their individual markings that much more distinct. Temperatures at the base of the Sawtooths can occasionally approach forty degrees below zero, but the wolves relished the cold. Curled up in the snow with noses tucked in their tails, they slept comfortably through the most bone-chilling winter nights.

The same could not be said for their human observers. The Dutchers offer tales of awaking to find their hair and pillows frozen solid, from the condensation of their breath, and of enduring days so cold that camera batteries died in minutes and audio cables became as stiff as tree branches. The Sawtooth Mountains shut out the western sky, shortening the already fleeting winter days. At 2:00 P.M. the sun slid behind the granite wall, leaving only an icy gray twilight. At such times, it was hopeless to attempt to film. All they could do was huddle around the woodstove in the yurt, busying themselves with small chores—cleaning gear, splitting wood, and work at keeping a clear path to the outhouse. The most laborious job of all was maintaining the supply of deer and elk for the hungry pack. With the blessing of Idaho's Department of Fish and Game, they collected the meat from the side of Highway 75, where roadkill is an unfortunate by-product of modern life, then hauled it back to camp by off-road vehicle or snowmobile.

Springtime brought more than relief from the weather. Certain years, the

arrival of spring meant the addition of new pups. Three of the four litters were introduced to the pack by the filmmakers. The final litter was provided by the Sawtooth Pack itself—born to Kamots and Chemukh, the alpha male and female. The wolf pups were in the company of humans from the moment they opened their eyes at ten days of age. Bottles of specially developed puppy formula served as mother's milk, and later, pureed chicken substituted for the partially digested meat that other members of a pack readily regurgitate for eager pups. Warm, damp rags simulated the licking and grooming of a mother's tongue, and just as often, those rags turned into toys for spirited bouts of tug-of-war.

During this crucial period, Jim and Jamie formed a deep relationship with the young pups that went far beyond simple habituation to humans. It was the kind of unshakable trust that wolves usually share only with their own pack—a bond that would last a lifetime. It is not only the force behind the Dutchers' success but also the very heart of their message.

"It was Kamots who really taught me about trust," Jim says. Kamots was the alpha male, the pack leader for most of his life. At the project's inception, however, he was a rambunctious ball of fur, frolicking with his littermates, attended to hand and foot by Jim and a handful of spellbound crew members. Dutcher had initially planned to start his own pack with two adult wolves, adding Kamots, his siblings, and a second litter of three males to make a family, but the approach failed. The adult female developed cataracts and, perhaps as a result of her being nearly blind (though no one is certain), the rest of the pack ostracized her completely. The

male, although having spent his life among people, regarded Jim as a stranger and never established that critical bond, reacting with nervousness and aggression that made him dangerous. Ultimately, both the male and female had to be relocated.

Jim shakes his head when he thinks back on those early days. "I realized then that I had made a big mistake. I had tried to jump-start the project by starting with adult wolves. I ended up learning the difference between a wolf that is merely habituated and a wolf that is really socialized—a wolf who has that trust." After the two adults had been relocated, Jim considered pulling the plug on the entire operation. But then, he says, a remarkable incident with Kamots changed his mind. "He had grown into a really beautiful, strong wolf. One day I was sitting by myself in the grass, pondering my options, when Kamots approached me, sat down beside me, and looked at me with his head cocked. Then he raised his paw and extended it toward me. He was the only one who had the confidence to do something like that." As he speaks, Jim kneels down in the meadow, demonstrating. "I held up my hand and he placed his paw against it. It felt at that moment as though we were making a sort of pact between us: If I would keep the project going, he would be the strong alpha the pack so desperately needed. In the years that followed, we each kept our promise."

Jim and Jamie continue to walk the familiar ground side by side, talking quietly and gesturing toward the sites of familiar scenes. Here, every natural feature is imbued with meaning: the pond where the wolves used to splash and play; the fiery red willows where Jamie first met Lakota, a wolf that became her favorite. Jamie

joined Jim halfway through the project (and subsequently married him), and the wolves took to her immediately. "You never know whether a wolf is going to accept you," she says. "But the pack had such a strong bond with Jim that, seeing me as his companion, I think it was easy for me to gain their trust." Shortly after her arrival, she joined in raising three new pups—two females and a male—to add to the five males who at the time made up what the Dutchers called the Sawtooth Pack.

In many ways, Jamie is the antithesis of Jim. While he is reserved and soft-spoken, she is warm and effervescent, with a ready laugh. Jamie has taken to the role of wolf advocate enthusiastically, often serving as the couple's public voice. Adamant in her calls for wilderness preservation and outspoken in her disapproval of pet wolves and wolf hybrids, she is seldom dispassionate when she speaks. She explains, "We talk about this trust, not just because it was so crucial to the project but because it is so important to understanding wolves. Seeing how wolves relate to one another, it is no mystery why the ancestors of our beloved dogs took to domestication so well. A dog—just like a wolf—craves companionship above all else." In dogs, this urge simply shifted to a relationship with a human master. In wolves, the bond is with the pack. Every wolf, from the alpha leader to the omega—the lowest-ranking member of wolf society—feels a sense of belonging. Only a special kind of wolf strikes out on its own and only under the right circumstances. But even then, it spends its time searching for another, following the scent trails, striving to end its loneliness and form a new pack.

"We don't know exactly how the wolves regarded us," Jamie continues. "It would be a stretch to say they thought of us as part of the pack, but our bond was something similar. They happily greeted us each day, and even after they were moved to the Nez Perce Reservation and our visits became less frequent, they continued to welcome us with the same enthusiasm. I think they just knew that we were loyal friends who had been with them from the beginning."

As they continue walking up the hill, Jamie's footsteps quicken as she makes a beeline for a dark tangle of spruce. Long ago, one of these massive trees toppled over. Under the great horizontal log is a narrow, dark cavern. In the entire wolf-camp area, this is the one remaining trace of the Sawtooth Pack: a den, dug by an expectant mother wolf nine years ago. Jamie is revisiting what was for her the most thrilling experience of her life with wolves.

She explains, "Chemukh was one of the pups I had raised. She was fairly submissive, nervous, and shy, but for some reason, as she grew into adulthood she began to assert herself, eventually winning the status of alpha female and the right to mate with Kamots. She started on several different dens, but in the end this was the site that suited her the most. When her time came, we just left her alone. We didn't try to follow her or film her. Several days later, we decided that it would be okay if I tried to crawl into the den to check on her pups. I sat with Chemukh for a while outside the den and talked to her softly, reassuring her and myself. Still, I wasn't sure whether she'd get scared and bite me on the rear when I was halfway in."

Jim chimes in, laughing. "Well, we never would have done it if it seemed to be upsetting Chemukh. One little growl from her and we would have stopped."

Jamie laughs too. "Really. Wolves have incredibly strong jaws. I wouldn't have taken the risk. But Chemukh was perfectly willing and even gave me a lick when I came back out. It goes back to my bonding with her as a pup. Her trust was absolute, and in reality, mine was too. Being able to peek in on her newborn pups—these tiny balls of fluff with their eyes shut tight, making these faint chirping sounds—what an incredible thrill! I knew I was witnessing something completely rare and beautiful and that it was a privilege that Chemukh granted to me."

By all accounts, the offspring of Kamots and Chemukh were the first wolves born in the area in sixty years. They weren't completely wild, of course, but they were born in nature, without human intervention, in a den dug by their mother. For the Dutchers, and for all who had eagerly awaited the return of wolves, the event was monumental, a harbinger of things to come. One year earlier in 1995, the U.S. Fish and Wildlife Service released more than a dozen wolves into the Frank Church–River of No Return Wilderness. Over the next few years, their ranks grew. Wolves dispersed and formed other packs. Some moved south into the White Cloud Mountains and, eventually, the Sawtooths. After the Dutchers' wolf camp was dismantled and the Sawtooth Pack had taken up new residence on the Nez Perce Reservation, wild wolves finally arrived to reclaim the land.

A wild wolf seldom lives beyond ten years; a captive wolf can sometimes live a few years longer. Born between 1991 and 1996, most of the Sawtooth Pack now exists only in memory. As the light begins to fade and the Dutchers make their way back down the slope toward their vehicle, Jim turns his thoughts away from the past. "This place belongs to the wild wolves now. We've even found tracks and scat right here. They probably investigated the old den and other traces that only they could detect. We now think of the Sawtooth Pack as ambassadors for their wild cousins. They didn't ask for that role, but they accepted it with more grace and beauty than I could ever have hoped for. Now it is up to us. If Jamie and I have achieved anything, people will be able to make the connection between the wolves they see in our films and books and the wild wolves they now hear about from politicians and the mainstream media. Even if all they hear are stories of 'dangerous beasts' and threats to livestock, hopefully now they know the other side."

Most of us will never see these new wild wolves. We may hear of them from time to time, identified with scientific detachment by the wildlife biologists who monitor them—"Yellowstone wolf #40" or "Idaho B24." They are elusive creatures, appearing, if at all, only as fleeting shadows. But from the stories, the images, and the sounds collected by Jim and Jamie Dutcher, we have an understanding now and a mental image. Through the lens of the Dutchers' work, forms take shape in the forest and individual personalities emerge: a confident alpha leading the pack in the hunt; a determined female striving for the right to breed; a concerned uncle giving up his own food so that the pack's young pups will have plenty; a resilient omega inciting the pack into a game of tag. We may never witness them chasing down an elk, hear their howls pierce the night air, or see their countless acts of care and devotion they display to one another, but we know them all the same.

They are the legacy of the Sawtooth Pack.

LEMUEL'S BLESSING

By William S. Merwin

Let Lemuel bless with the wolf, which is a dog without a master, but the Lord hears his cries and feeds him in the desert.
Christopher Smart, *Jubilate Agno*

You that know the way,
Spirit,
I bless your ears which are like cypresses on a mountain
With their roots in wisdom. Let me approach.
I bless your paws and their twenty nails which tell their own prayer
And are like dice in command of their own combinations.
Let me not be lost.
I bless your eyes for which I know no comparison.
Run with me like the horizon, for without you
I am nothing but a dog lost and hungry,
Ill-natured, untrustworthy, useless.

My bones together bless you like an orchestra of flutes.
Divert the weapons of the settlements and lead their dogs a dance.
Where a dog is shameless and wears servility
In his tail like a banner,
Let me wear the opprobrium of possessed and possessors
As a thick tail properly used
To warm my worst and my best parts. My tail and my laugh bless you.
Lead me past the error at the fork of hesitation.
Deliver me

From the ruth of the lair, which clings to me in the morning,
Painful when I move, like a trap;
Even debris has its favorite positions but they are not yours;
From the ruth of kindness, with its licked hands;
I have sniffed baited fingers and followed
Toward necessities which were not my own: it would make me
An habitué of back steps, faithful custodian of fat sheep;

From the ruth of prepared comforts, with its
Habitual dishes sporting my name and its collars and leashes of vanity;

From the ruth of approval, with its nets, kennels, and taxidermists;
It would use my guts for its own rackets and instruments, to play its
    own games and music;
Teach me to recognize its platforms, which are constructed like
    scaffolds;

From the ruth of known paths, which would use my feet, tail, and ears
    as curios,
My head as a nest for tame ants,
My fate as a warning.

I have hidden at wrong times for wrong reasons.
I have been brought to bay. More than once.
Another time, if I need it,
Create a little wind like a cold finger between my shoulders, then
Let my nails pour out a torrent of aces like grain from a threshing machine;
Let fatigue, weather, habitation, the old bones, finally,
Be nothing to me,
Let all lights but yours be nothing to me.
Let the memory of tongues not unnerve me so that I stumble or quake.

But lead me at times beside the still waters;
There when I crouch to drink let me catch a glimpse of your image
Before it is obscured with my own.

Preserve my eyes, which are irreplaceable.
Preserve my heart, veins, bones,
Against the slow death building in them like hornets until the place is entirely theirs.
Preserve my tongue and I will bless you again and again.

Let my ignorance and my failings
Remain far behind me like tracks made in a wet season,
At the end of which I have vanished,
So that those who track me for their own twisted ends
May be rewarded only with ignorance and failings.
But let me leave my cry stretched out behind me like a road
On which I have followed you.
And sustain me for the time in the desert
On what is essential to me.

Living with Wolves

philosophy

When Jim Dutcher began his film documentary project on wolves, there were only about fifty wild wolves left in the entire American West. Over the previous two centuries, more than two million wolves had been poisoned, shot, or trapped. One of the legendary noble creatures of the wilderness was headed straight for extinction.

Already cautious and elusive by nature, wolves have learned to fear and avoid humans, making it all but impossible to get close enough to observe and photograph them. A chance glimpse of this animal in its wild habitat is a rare and thrilling event. Photographing wolves in the wild can also cause unsettling disturbances in their behavior and problems with their well-being. A wild wolf that has become habituated to humans doesn't have long to live—the next time someone points an object at that wolf, it might be a gun instead of a camera.

∽

JIM: *In filming the wolf, our goal was to observe not as scientists but as social partners. I knew from years of experience as a nature cinematographer that even seeing a wolf in the wild is a rare occurrence. Getting them to reveal their social structure, their manner of communication, and their intimate family life would require special conditions. I wanted to come as close as humanly possible to experiencing life inside a wolf pack. Although the politics, science, and history of wolves are fascinating subjects, my intention was to show their inner lives and inner workings and to understand their essence.*

FILMING THE WOLVES ON THEIR TERMS

Building on his previous experiences as a wildlife cinematographer and in consultation with biologists and wolf experts, Jim's solution was to form his own pack of wolves. He acquired four pups that were ten days old and set out to socialize them to be unaffected by the presence of humans. Acting as surrogate parents, Jim and his crew simulated a mother's care as best they could by using warm, damp rags to imitate her tongue and by holding the pups in blankets to replicate her body heat and fur. Jim and his team fed the young wolf pups a specially modified canine puppy formula every four to six hours, and after a

feeding the pups would fall asleep in their laps. Jim and his crew worked shifts so someone was with the pups at all times.

These intense sessions formed the basis for gaining the trust of the wolves—a relationship that grew into a lifelong bond. On the edge of the Idaho wilderness, Jim and his team enclosed acres of stream, forest, and meadow, providing ample space and freedom for the wolves to live as a fully functional pack. For six continuous years, they camped among the wolves, observing and photographing their fascinating behavior, antic play, and complex social life.

❧

JIM: *We are not scientists. Although we tried to remain pragmatic, we bonded with the wolves as much as they bonded with us. Our accounts are based on our feelings and experiences as filmmakers and as human beings. This perspective allowed us a range of speculation that might make a scientist uncomfortable. We were, however, extremely careful not to be swayed by fantasy or to make the wolves out to be more than they are. In the end, they are neither demons nor deities, but incredible and inspiring creatures in their own right. We set out to capture their lives on film and to show a side of them that is often overlooked by scientists and politicians. What we ultimately experienced went well beyond our expectations. They opened up their lives to us and accepted us as part of their world.*

34

logistics: the setting

The ground is abundant with willow and grass, braided by numerous small streams. One side of a wide, pretty meadow is bordered by a grove of aspen, and a cool mountain brook flows along the other. Lodgepole pine and spruce form a deeply forested area; in the background soar the majestic granite walls of the Sawtooth Mountains. The spectacular alpine terrain of central Idaho was about to become home to a unique pack of wolves and to an ambitious film documentary project. The logistics for the project fell into place, but not without a great deal of explanation, patience, and persistence. Public apprehension and encumbering bureaucracy dogged every step.

The project was envisioned at a contentious time when the U.S. government was beginning to choose areas around the United States where wolves would be reintroduced. One of the areas selected was the Frank Church–River of No Return Wilderness, just to the north of the Sawtooth Range. Many local ranchers and hunters reacted to the federal project by adopting what was referred to as a "shoot, shovel, and shut up" policy toward the wolves.

Nonetheless, the U.S. Forest Service issued permits to set up the camp and the twenty-five-acre wolf enclosure. The Idaho Department of Fish and Game approved the permits required to keep wolves—an endangered species—for a documentary film and research project. Even more surprising, three ranchers graciously allowed access to the new wolf camp via their property, proof that some were more intrigued by the project than alarmed. As touchy as the situation was in the early 1990s, it is even more deeply polarized today. A complicated, interdependent project on wolves of this magnitude surely would be impossible to re-create in the current political climate.

❧

WOLF CAMP

JIM: *My production assistant for my first wolf documentary,* Wolf: Return of a Legend, *was a mountain guide and avalanche expert who introduced us to winter survival skills and also to a type of tent called a yurt, which originated among the nomads of Mongolia. This round, sixteen-foot-diameter structure featured a*

conical roof sturdy enough to withstand the pressure of several feet of snow. Three additional tents accommodated our needs and included space for occasional visitors. I wanted to create an environment that contributed to resourceful thinking, where a well-organized working and living space left our minds free to concentrate on our work. What could have been merely a functional base camp became a special place and a comfortable home for the better part of six years.

The yurt served as the communal area and extra sleeping quarters, although there were rarely more than four people at wolf camp at any given time. The logistics of camp life were rigorous and the care of the pack was a continuous commitment. Filmmaking, sound recording, and photography also were full-time jobs.

At first located outside the wolves' territory, the tents and the yurt were elevated on eight-inch-high platforms to minimize impact to the landscape, as well as to allow for water that coursed through the camp when snow began to melt in the spring. Each tent also had a small woodstove. The facilities were simple, efficient, and comfortable, with firewood for heat, candles for light, and propane for cooking. The creek or melted snow provided wash water. Any "extravagances" resulted from either hard work or innovation: a table where the crew could eat together, a shower area, comfortable beds—a good night's sleep

being a necessity for facing a cold, strenuous day of work. The extra effort of packing in a heavy bottle of wine or two when resupplying always met with universal approval.

∽

JIM: *Several seasons into the project, Jamie and I decided to move inside the wolves' territory, to live as directly as we could with the animals. Logistics were kept as simple as possible. Our "inside" camp consisted of a small tent for sleeping and the yurt, now raised on an eight-foot-high platform that provided storage space underneath and a wonderful high vantage point to film the pack from. It was a little enclosure for people inside the larger enclosure for the wolves. To minimize distractions for the wolves, the other tents remained outside. The yurt became the center for communal life, where we gathered for meals and shared our experiences and observations.*

The benefits of this new setup were immediate. Instead of entering the wolves' territory through the noisy gate every morning, we simply walked down the stairs from our yurt, minimizing our disturbance of the pack. This increased closeness to the wolves revealed greater subtleties of body language and nuances of behavior. I had filmed wild wolves in Alaska and Yellowstone, but I had never been able to film the complex, fascinating social interchange that was revealed to us by living among the Sawtooth Pack.

The Life of a Wolf Pack

introducing the members of the sawtooth pack

∾

JIM: Fifty years after the last wild wolf was heard howling in the Idaho wilderness, we assembled the beginnings of our pack. Like surrogate parents, we bottle-fed these pups from the day they opened their eyes in order to establish a complete trust with them. For six years we lived with the wolves, filming, recording their sounds, and studying their behavior on an intimate scale. The photographs in this book were selected from more than 14,000 images taken during this time. For our own reference, we gave the wolves names, using the Lakota Sioux, Blackfoot, and Nez Perce languages to describe qualities that might characterize a wolf. Because the wolves were wild animals, we never tried to teach them their names. In any case, by nature the wolves would not respond to being summoned by name as a domestic pet would.

KAMOTS (Kuh-MOTZ)

Blackfoot for "freedom"

Alpha male

The most confident wolf and the leader of the entire pack, Kamots was the most vigilant, first to respond to strange sounds and smells or to potential threats to the group. Curious and tolerant, he led with intelligence and benevolence.

CHEMUKH (cha-MUCK)

Nez Perce for "black lassie"

Alpha female

In the Nez Perce language, the names for colors are repeated twice, so at first this skittish dark female was called Chemukh-Chemukh Ayet, for "black lassie." We quickly abbreviated the name to Chemukh. Her nervous, loner behavior as a puppy seemed to destine her for an omega role. It came as a complete surprise when she asserted herself and was accepted by Kamots as his mate. She gave birth to three pups—Piyip and his sisters Ayet and Motaki.

MATSI (MOT-zee)

Blackfoot for "sweet and brave"

Beta male

Matsi was the beta wolf—second in command. Betas are always subordinate to the alpha and dominate the mid-ranking and omega wolves. In addition, Matsi had a capacity for caring that is not necessarily an inherent beta trait. In the Sawtooth Pack, Matsi was the peacemaker and devoted babysitter who helped discipline and raise the pups. His distinguishing marks included a golden rather than gray mask.

WYAKIN (Why-AH-kin)

Nez Perce for "spirit guide to children"

Omega female

A *wyakin* is a guardian spirit said to come to Nez Perce children during vigils, revealing truths about life and teaching special songs. The only other female in the pack, and subordinate to her sister Chemukh, Wyakin was a light-colored wolf with a playful and sweet disposition.

MOTOMO (Muh-TOE-moe)

Blackfoot for "he who goes first"

Mid-rank

The brother of Matsi, Motomo was a coal-black wolf—mild mannered, yet aggressive on a kill. Demanding of attention, he usually achieved goals through persistence or mischievousness. His watchful and mysterious presence was accentuated by striking yellow eyes.

AMANI (Uh-MA-knee)

Blackfoot for "speaking the truth"

Mid-rank

A brother of Matsi and Motomo, Amani was generally mild and gentle, preferring eating, sleeping, or playing the clown to the rigors of jostling for social rank. He was often at odds with his brother Motomo. When the pups Piyip, Ayet, and Motaki were born, he took on the role of indulgent uncle. He had the classic gray wolf coloring.

52

WAHOTS (Wah-HOTZ)

Nez Perce for "likes to howl"

Mid-rank

Wahots was the brother of Chemukh and Wyakin. With a large head and almond-shaped eyes, he was one of the most elegant and photogenic members of the pack. Although there was no way to predict his personality when he was named, Wahots did end up being one of the most vocal members of the pack. After the aging Lakota was allowed to retire from the omega role, Wahots was forced into this lowly rank.

LAKOTA (Lah-COAT-ah)

Lakota Sioux for "friend"

Omega male

Lakota, the brother of Kamots, spent most of his years as the omega, the lowest-ranking member of the pack. Although equal in size to Kamots, Lakota continually held himself in a submissive pose so as not to attract attention and disapproval from the rest of the pack. Ever the scapegoat and always the last to feed, he nonetheless had a positive influence on the pack by regularly initiating play.

JAMIE: *From the start of the project, Jim knew that these wolves could never be set free. A habituated wolf, having lost its fear of humans, could possibly gravitate toward human activities and get into trouble. People's fear and suspicion would give any habituated wolf a slim chance of survival. Knowing that the permit to stay on U.S. Forest Service land would eventually expire, Jim had formed an organization to create a new home for the pack.*

When the Nez Perce tribe offered to lease a parcel of land in northern Idaho for these wolves, we were overjoyed. Working with the tribe, we built a new home for the pack on Nez Perce land, similar in size to their old territory in the Sawtooths, preparing for a day that would inevitably arrive. The pack was moved in 1996, but our bond with the wolves remains strong, and our resolve to continue telling their story and our unique experience is a lifelong commitment for us.

54

hierarchy: organization of a wolf pack

Like a human being, a wolf bases its life on a social structure of family and community. Examination of the social behavior of wolves reveals a sophisticated and caring animal whose well-being results from an interdependent and complex social system.

Based on strong family ties and allegiances, the pack is held together by trust, instinct, and the DNA of thousands of years of evolved wolf society. A pack is an extended family of brothers, sisters, aunts, and uncles. Led by the alpha male and alpha female, pack life is ordered around a strictly enforced social hierarchy in which every wolf has a specific rank and role. The hierarchy among mid-ranking wolves seems fluid and prone to frequent shifts. On the other hand, the roles of alpha and omega—the top and bottom of the hierarchy—are usually fixed. They seldom change except under serious conditions such as the death or injury of another pack member.

A hierarchy with clearly established leadership also offers the best chance for a successful hunt, with each member playing a mutually supportive role. Over tens of thousands of years, wolves evolved this survival strategy of sustaining each individual by performing as a team. Not collaborating could mean a missed meal. And there is safety in numbers—an orchestrated attack with many wolves acting as one synchronized organism enables them to take down large game such as moose or elk and lessens the ever-present risk of serious injury.

However, the social hierarchy is about more than just competition and hunting strategy. Wolves develop trust in one another from lifelong bonds that reinforce a sense that they *belong* to a particular family and a specific pack. Cooperation extends into other aspects of their social life: rearing young, caring for injured members, defending territory.

The pack hierarchy generally has parallel lines of dominance for each sex. The alpha male dominates the entire pack. The beta, or second-rank, wolf dominates the mid-ranking wolves, also called subordinates. All adult wolves dominate the wolves in the lowest position—the omega male and omega female.

Although this social structure is strict, in that there will always be an alpha, a beta, and an omega—with numerous mid-ranking wolves—a wolf's

specific position within the hierarchy can change with circumstances. An aging alpha with diminished health may be forced to retire, his once-confident demeanor replaced by sudden deference to a new leader. A scrappy and aggressive beta may then assume the alpha role and evolve more altruistic and relaxed traits befitting a leader. However, holding the beta position—"second in command"—does not automatically assure a wolf succession to the alpha role. In the Sawtooth Pack, for example, Matsi's beta rank was secure only as long as Kamots remained the alpha. The pack is an interdependent entity, and the reasons for position within the pack are complex and not always predictable or understood, except by the wolves themselves.

Interestingly, the stereotypical "lone wolf" is something of a romantic myth. In reality, a wolf is lost without the social context of a pack. Naturalists prefer to use the term "disperser" for a wolf that leaves its pack and strikes out on its own—a rare and usually temporary condition. A disperser is typically a young wolf that is unable or unwilling to assimilate into the pack hierarchy. It may feel compelled to be the leader of its own pack or want to escape its status as a subordinate wolf. Dispersers may follow their former pack for some time, begin a pack of their own with another disperser, or, in rare instances, even join another pack. Biologists in Yellowstone were surprised when a male disperser from the Rose Creek Pack was not only accepted into the Druid Pack but also immediately awarded alpha status.

In any case, a disperser remains driven to reestablish some kind of pack

bond and end its solitary existence. A wolf's survival depends on its being part of a pack, and the mortality rate of loners is extremely high. However, the risky undertaking of a disperser striking out on its own ensures that genetic diversity will be maintained, and therefore it is vital to the health of the species.

ALPHA

Traditionally, the alpha male is the supreme leader of the entire pack, but there are also instances in which an alpha female may lead a pack. The alpha male and female are the primary decision makers. They are the first to deal with outside threats to the pack or to assess new circumstances, sounds, and smells.

There are two particular occasions when the hierarchy within a pack is most apparent. One is during feeding, when the alpha decides and enforces who eats first and who eats last. The other is during breeding season, when dominant males and females aggressively display their status. Typically, the alpha pair is the sole breeding couple in the pack. Occasionally, depending on circumstances such as availability of prey, an alpha male may mate with another female member of the pack or allow the beta male to mate with a beta or a subordinate female.

Leadership manifests itself as both autocratic—with pack members dependent on the leader for direction—as well as democratic, when the leader appears to take cues from other pack members and then makes decisions accordingly. The qualities of the alpha leader are critical to the survival of the community. Packs led by benevolent, confident leaders are the most

harmonious and efficient, with the greatest chance for survival.

Leadership traits can show up early in life. Kamots held the alpha position in the Sawtooth Pack from the time he was an adolescent. However, fights for the dominant alpha role can be brutal, and there may be many confrontations before the role becomes firmly established. Kamots carried himself with confidence— holding his head and ears up and his tail high to signify dominance. During ritual greetings, the other pack members lavished attention on Kamots and displayed appropriate submission by licking his face and keeping their heads and tails lower than his. They whined and crouched low to the ground, while he growled to affirm his superior status. This is not a wanton display of power politics—it is the social glue that keeps pack members bonded to each other.

BETA

The beta wolf is the "second in command," dominant over all but the alpha. If the current alpha is killed or injured, the beta male may assume command of the pack, if he displays the leadership qualities intrinsic to the role. For this reason, a beta may have to perform the most delicate balancing act of any wolf within the society: ready to assume a leadership role, yet remaining loyal to the existing alpha.

MID-RANK (SUBORDINATE)

Although the alpha, beta, and omega wolves are clearly defined as individuals, the rest of the adult pack members are referred to simply as "mid-ranking." It is difficult for an observer to determine the precise pecking order within the middle ranks, but there is little doubt that the wolves themselves know, for in a wolf pack there are never any equals. The status of any wolf can change, and this is especially true in the middle ranks, where life can be quite tumultuous on a continual basis.

Within the Sawtooth Pack, Amani and Motomo seemed especially prone to flip-flops in their status. One day Amani would display clear dominance, climbing on Motomo's back and growling menacingly. The next day Motomo would be chasing his brother off a kill.

PUPS AND ADOLESCENTS

Indulged and adored by the adults, pups hold a special status within the pack. For a time, they exist outside the pack hierarchy. They are submissive to the adults, but they are also coddled and allowed to feed alongside the most dominant adults. A litter of pups will work out its own separate hierarchy, though the ranks they establish at this stage may be fleeting.

When they become adolescents and begin to assimilate into the adult hierarchy, their "pup hierarchy" evaporates amid new dynamics and new allegiances. When a pack has many adult wolves and a solidly established hierarchy, a young wolf might maintain puppy status for as long as two years, sometimes even longer. ▷

OMEGA

Opposite from the alpha is the omega, the bottom rung of pack hierarchy. The omega must constantly yield to all the other adult wolves, living a difficult existence at the fringe of pack life. While the alpha male and female "earn" their position, the omega has its role forced on it by the rest of the pack. Eventually the pack may allow the omega to retire, turning its aggression toward another wolf. At that point the old omega will move aside, though it never ascends very high within the social structure.

The omega fulfills the role of the pack scapegoat—always the last to eat, always receiving the brunt of pack aggression. No other position in the pack requires as much talent for diplomacy and appeasement. Through this trial of constant abuse, omegas often become resourceful. They frequently use games and play to divert aggression and diffuse conflicts. Nonetheless, the omega endures considerable physical mistreatment and ostracism.

Although the omega's unfortunate status is largely beyond its control, wolves in this position seem to be born with certain timid and submissive qualities that make them suited to the role. Although the lowest rank, the omega is nonetheless a solid position within the pack and so carries with it a sense of belonging.

❧

JAMIE: *One of the first things I noticed when I met Lakota was his posture. As the omega, he kept his tail tucked, his shoulders hunched, and his head lowered as he moved uncertainly toward me. It wasn't until he reached me that I realized he was a huge wolf, possibly even larger than his brother, Kamots, the alpha, although his submissive posture made it difficult to discern this when they were together. Lakota's paws were definitely bigger. If size and strength were the determining factors to dominance, he would have been a very high-ranking wolf. Clearly, there is a lot more to the social hierarchy than we currently understand.*

As Lakota reached me and timidly licked my face, I ran my hand down his back through his new winter coat. His skin was riddled with small bumps and scabs where the other wolves had nipped him, and there were small scars on his muzzle where the fur would not grow back. As I sat quietly with him, he started to relax, beginning to trust that I wasn't going to hurt him. He then did an extraordinary thing: he gently placed his paw on my shoulder and gazed at me directly with his sweet, wise amber eyes. We stayed that way for quite some time. From that moment, I was captivated by him and would forever hold a special place for him in my heart.

Over the years, Lakota and I continued to have this special bond. Sometimes I would sneak away from the rest of the pack to carry on this secret friendship with the beleaguered omega, out of sight of the other wolves. I was careful not to show any interest in him when the rest of the pack was nearby, and he seemed to do the same with me, to avoid the painful risk of being disciplined by one of the mid-ranking wolves. Instead, I would join Lakota when he was by himself, and we would sit together with his paw on my shoulder, as we had done the first time we met.

raising young pups

Mating occurs once a year in February or March, and females give birth two months later to a litter averaging four to seven pups. The size of the litter and how many pups survive depend on the food supply, the weather, and the health and age of the mother. About half the pups born will usually succumb to predators, disease, and natural attrition.

Although pups are typically born to the alpha male and female, they belong to the group as a whole, as part of an extended family. All members of the pack have a role to play in the pups' upbringing, including protecting, feeding, educating, and disciplining them.

∽

JAMIE: *As the faint whimpers of new life drifted out of the opening to Chemukh's den, the Sawtooth Pack paced nervously with an air of great excitement and anticipation. Just days after the birth, Chemukh, the mother, emerged from the den and greeted me with a reassuring lick to the face. I sat among the pack, recording the sounds of the new pups, and spoke quietly to Chemukh. Jim was filming me at the time and I remember looking up at him. With a nod, he indicated to me that the time seemed right to proceed with what we had planned. Withdrawing a small flashlight from my pocket, I showed the foreign object to Chemukh to establish that it posed no danger.*

Getting down on hands and knees, I crawled headfirst down into the den, inhaling the sweet fragrance of the damp spring earth. The narrow tunnel was about five feet long, bearing to the left around a tree root. I emerged into a wide area with a slight rise at one end, and then there were the pups, all huddled together. I had read about wolves leaving a section of the den elevated to protect the pups from any water that might collect on the floor. It certainly made me wonder if Chemukh understood the underlying mechanics behind the construction or was acting purely on instinct.

I spent only a few brief minutes with this fragile bundle of new life, emerging from the den to a reassuring lick on the nose from Chemukh before she disappeared down the hole to check on her young. She did not extend visiting privileges to the other wolves, so it was quite an honor that she allowed me this encounter. I was intensely moved by this expression of friendship and trust. ▷

At birth, the pups weigh about a pound each, with eyes tightly shut; they are also nearly deaf. They are completely reliant on their mother. At around ten days, the pups begin to open their eyes.

The mother begins to wean her pups from her milk when they're about four weeks old; she rejoins the hunt, leaving the pups behind with another pack member acting as a babysitter. At this point, all members of the pack assume responsibility for feeding the pups. When the pack returns from the hunt, the pups instinctively rush to their elders, begging for food, and lick the mouths of the adults. This stimulates the adults to regurgitate partially digested meat, food that the pups can easily digest themselves.

At about six weeks, wolf pups begin tentatively to explore the world outside their den on their own. Although as pups they live outside the social hierarchy of the adults, even at this young age they display dominant and submissive behavior and vie for social status among themselves. The exercise helps the pups develop the social skills necessary to integrate with the rest of the pack as they mature.

∽

JIM: *After feeding the pups, we spent time playing and talking softly with them. Sometimes the play turned rough, and we would restrain or discipline the pups, adopting and mimicking the language and traditions of wolf society. Rolling the pup over on its back into the belly-up submissive position for a few seconds usually restored the peace. On some occasions, however, this was not enough and, just as a wolf parent would do, we would reinstate order by sternly issuing a low-pitched growl. We always treated the wolves with tenderness and respect and made every effort to allow them to establish their own society and sort out their own differences.*

The pups grow and begin to participate in the rewards of a hunt at about twelve weeks of age. Subordinate adult wolves often have to wait to eat until both the dominant members of the pack, as well as the pups, have had their fill. Wolf pups grow quite rapidly, putting on an average of three pounds a week for the first three months of their lives. A young wolf must capitalize on this growth before winter so it can keep up with the rest of the pack, particularly in deep snow. After six months, the pups are almost as big as the senior members of the pack, although their softer fur, slighter stature, and frolicsome spirit give them away as juveniles for another year or more.

Pups idolize and mimic the adults—walking, eating, sniffing, and chewing on everything the adults do. In this way, knowledge is passed from generation to generation. Pups learn quickly, and as adolescents, they begin to assimilate into the adult hierarchy in their second year. Much of a wolf's social position depends on the confidence it displays right from the beginning. Just as human children playing on a school playground open themselves up to bullying if they behave in a meek or submissive manner, fear or timidity in a young wolf will often destine the wolf to a lower position in the pecking order. ▷

The Sawtooth Pack was originally assembled with two adults, plus
four pups. Over the course of the project's six years, six more pups were
introduced at various intervals. An alpha pair emerged—Kamots and
Chemukh—who eventually mated, and Chemukh gave birth to an
additional three surviving pups.

collaboration on the hunt

Wolves have evolved skills and attributes that make them among the most admired hunters in the animal world. Their keen sense of smell is estimated to be a hundred times more acute than that of humans, allowing them to detect prey more than a mile away. On open ground, they have been observed responding to sounds emanating from more than ten miles away. Although wolves have superior night vision compared with humans and greater perception concerning motion, they are unable to focus on objects more than seventy-five feet away. Their superior senses, evolved for hunting, enable them to hide themselves from prey until they are ready to be seen.

∽

JAMIE: *Wolves have a nearly magical ability to vanish into their surroundings or to appear suddenly as if out of thin air. On numerous occasions, as we walked through the woods, we would be completely unable to find the wolves. After a while, one wolf would unexpectedly appear from the shadows, then another, until the entire pack came into view. We realized that they had probably been traveling just a few yards away, watching us for quite some time. Just as quickly as they materialized, they would melt back into the landscape and become invisible once again.*

Wolves' primary advantage, however, is not individual attributes but the "power of the pack," wherein each individual has a specific, complementary role to play. Native people tell of watching how wolves hunt and developing similar hunting strategies based on the strength of the group over the relative weakness of a single individual. Wolves are the only animals in North America that consistently hunt in a pack. They will take up positions to stalk, herd, run down and kill their prey, coordinating individual skills and strengths relative to the other pack members. Observers report that often the smaller, swifter females act as herders and flankers, while the larger, more powerful males often initiate the actual takedown. The wolves share decision making, and there is surprising flexibility in their roles. Even juveniles will join in the hunt, learning to herd and tackle by mimicking the more experienced wolves. Watching a pack hunt is like watching a single organism at work—an elegant, nearly

telepathic orchestration of synchronized motion and focused intent.

Wolves develop strategies and tactics based on a number of variables, including the availability and condition of the prey, the weather, the terrain, and the season of year. In fair weather, they can often subsist on small game that may be hunted individually, such as rabbits and ground squirrels. Larger game requires the full participation and cooperation of the group.

In winter, wolves have a distinct advantage over ungulates such as deer, elk, moose, and caribou, whose slim hooves will cut through crusty, deep snow, greatly impeding their efficiency and speed. In contrast, wolves' paws are large pads that act like snowshoes—allowing the wolves to move on the top of the snow with significantly less effort and greater speed than their targeted prey. Even in soft, deep snow, a wolf has an additional advantage: its narrow chest acts like the prow of a ship, cutting much of the resistance.

During caribou migrations, wolves may travel with the herd for days before making a move. They scan the caribou for young, injured, old, or sick prey. They would much rather take a weak member of the herd, because the kill would be physically less exhausting and potentially less risky. Wolves can easily be injured by powerful hooves and sharp antlers, and so they prefer to take as few risks as possible. Of course, as necessity and opportunity dictate, they won't hesitate to take down a healthy animal.

Wolves have evolved with a sense of ecological balance and are self-regulating, mating and breeding as necessary to maintain optimum pack size.

How large the pack is allowed to get depends primarily on the availability of food and space—factors tied directly to location. A Canadian pack that may hunt bison, moose, or caribou would have to be much larger to take down its sizable prey, whereas a Montana pack, with limited space but plentiful small white-tailed deer, would do better with fewer members. Packs numbering twenty wolves or more have been reported in remote parts of Alaska.

Wolves can consume as much as twenty-five to thirty pounds in a feeding and will go for days without eating again. Wolves eat almost every part of their prey, including bones, hooves, and internal organs. Adult wolves will go hungry if necessary so that young pups may eat. The ability of the pack as a whole to meet the individual needs of each member is crucial to pack survival. Although the alpha wolf directs pack activities, the pack also works as a unit, with all ranks contributing to the group's overall decisions. A wolf pack is very similar to a human family, wherein strengths, abilities, and personality traits are all important elements that enable the unit to compete and flourish.

wolf play

Snarls and nips, running and chasing, flipping and rolling: any of these behaviors can indicate a fight for dominance or a high-spirited session of play. In a bout of play, just enough restraint is used to avoid causing harm.

Play is a crucial component in every stage of a wolf's life, and it is the one time when the strict hierarchy of the pack may be temporarily suspended. Pups may pounce and chew on an adult without discipline (unless the session gets out of control and requires a bit of subduing).

Soon after birth, wolf pups climb and roll over each other, foretelling future rounds of dominance struggles. As the pups grow, play becomes the primary tool for learning skills and handling aggression. It is also great exercise: reflexes develop and muscles toughen during these vigorous bouts of wrestling, chasing, and chewing. Siblings play as a group and take turns sneaking up on each other or "subduing" sticks and branches in preparation for the day when they will employ these skills on a real hunt. After countless hours of play, each wolf's physicality—its relative strengths and weaknesses and its style of motion—is etched into the minds of its pack mates. Thus they can, when needed, move together in perfect synchronization.

Young wolves frequently engage in "jaw sparring," in which one wolf will try to hold another wolf's muzzle between its teeth in mock combat. In a game similar to thumb wrestling, one wolf will glower and growl while attempting to clamp down on another's muzzle. In doing so, they develop proficiencies they will need as they mature and compete for status within the pack ranking. Adult wolves, too, engage in jaw sparring as a relatively benign way of establishing or reinforcing the pack hierarchy.

Any event can spark wolf play. Even falling snow can cause the pack to erupt in a spontaneous celebratory romp. They may chase each other or nip at a tail or rump as they take turns being the pursuer and the pursued. During play, the tensions created by the firm hierarchy of pack society seem to lessen and wolves may temporarily reverse social roles. During such times, even the omega can chase and nip at the dominant alpha without fear of reprisal. ▷

JAMIE: Whether by themselves or in the company of other pack members, wolves play with a variety of objects: branches, sticks, rocks, and clumps of hide can serve as toys. During filming, anything not nailed down was fair game—often never to be seen again or seen again in barely recognizable bits and pieces. Lens caps, gloves, tools, and, especially, my hat were all hotly coveted. Kamots was notorious for his stalking and stealthy confiscation of these prizes. Once in possession of the new treasure, he would prance about, playfully tossing and displaying the new item—daring people and wolves alike to "come and get it."

Often, the omega wolf acts like a court jester to lighten the mood of the pack. Lakota would grab a stick or an old bone, sometimes twirling it like a baton over his head, and race off into the meadow, inviting the others to chase him. The thrill of the game was usually enough to get the others to join in readily. Lakota often coaxed Kamots into a game of tag in which the alpha and omega both took turns being "it." Scientists might disdain the thought of assigning emotions to an animal, but since I'm not a scientist, I have no trouble calling it the way I see it. Witnessing scenes of play such as this, it appeared to me that the usual grimace of the beleaguered omega was replaced with what looked like a smile of pure joy.

Many years later, while filming through the open door of a small airplane, Jim and I watched a pack of wolves along the Yukon River. The wolves were engaged in a spirited game of tag, and I was caught in the reverie of similar moments with the

Sawtooth Pack. As the wolves below chased and nipped each other's tails, I could imagine their expressions of joy. I knew that one of the wolves below me was the omega, keeping the tradition of the game alive.

The Inner Wolf

communication

BODY LANGUAGE: EMOTIONS

Acting on inspiration, Jim decided to film the wolves in slow motion to better capture their grace and beauty. However, this technique ended up providing much more than just beautiful footage. Because many of the nuances of a wolf's behavior happen so quickly, they are difficult to see in real time, so filming in slow motion suddenly revealed swift gestures such as a quick cock of the head or a brief flash of fang. Reviewing these scenes frame by frame, Jim and Jamie were able to examine subtle interactions that they had failed to notice earlier.

Wolves continually communicate with each other, sorting out their social positions and reinforcing the stability of the pack. For example, one wolf resting its head over the top of another wolf's back is a sign of affection, but it is also a gentle indication of dominance. Certain sounds or gestures find unmistakable parallels in human communication; others defy all attempts at translation.

The range of vocalizations, body language, facial expressions, personalities, and behaviors that Jim and Jamie witnessed and recorded over the years coalesced to suggest an intricate and rich emotional component to the inner life of wolves.

Jamie believes her experiences with the Sawtooth Pack provide not only a glimpse into the private lives of wolves but also a way for her to better comprehend her own humanity. The validity of interpreting the emotions of a wolf is, of course, open to argument, and a scientist may steadfastly resist this temptation. Most scientists will allow, however, that wolves do appear to express complex feelings.

The wolf hierarchy exhibits displays of care, empathy, and collaboration as well as contention. The Dutchers observed and filmed ferocious behavior associated with establishing and maintaining pack hierarchy, but they also witnessed and recorded traits that humans admire, including the extremely affectionate and playful behavior associated with bonding as a family unit. Few animals on earth display the same intensity of commitment to family in the collaborative care of their young. Expressions of joy are evident at the birth of new pups, as are those of sorrow when a pack member dies. Play, complex in its rules and manifestations, is essential to the emotional stability of the pack.

Jim recalls how Motaki, the earliest pack omega (whose name would later be given to one of Chemukh's pups), was a submissive and sometimes fearful

scapegoat of the pack. Yet she had an endearing ability to inspire the most spirited bouts of play. She seemed to organize games in part to deflect abuse away from herself. In any case, her role was critical to the cohesion and well-being of the pack.

One unforgettable morning, Jim made a terrible discovery. Motaki had been killed by a mountain lion that had managed to scale the fence and enter the enclosure. For the six weeks that followed her death, the pack did not play. What had been a daily occurrence stopped altogether. When the wolves passed through the aspen grove where she had been killed, they became quiet, their tails drooping noticeably. When they howled, Jim noted that the sound had an eerie quality, very different from the normal riotous pack rallies. Jim could come to only one conclusion: the wolves were in mourning.

All the wolves displayed great sensitivity and often acted with a unified mood. For the filmmakers, however, one particular pack member embodied all the qualities that humans find so admirable in wolves. This was Matsi, the ever-dutiful beta wolf.

∽

JIM: *As I reflect on our years of living with the Sawtooth Pack, Matsi, the beta, embodied all that was magical about them. Matsi patrolled their territory and took a central role in the care of the pups—almost exhausting himself keeping track of all of them and regurgitating half his food to keep them well fed. He maintained peace and order in the pack—and amid all this, he seemed completely content not to rule. Although competition among pack members is prevalent, Matsi always had the good*

of the pack in mind. Through Matsi, I realized that the workings of a wolf society are deeper and more complex than I could ever imagine.

Matsi possessed an intangible quality that is still difficult to describe. He always conducted himself with calm dignity. For Matsi, the well-being of the pack was paramount—the cohesion of the family was more important than anything. He wasn't terribly concerned with what we humans were up to, but he did seem to enjoy our company. Sometimes he would come and sit beside me—never actively soliciting my attention, never expecting anything, just spending time with a friend.

When I filmed the pack during the mayhem of feeding and then reviewed the many separate incidents in slow motion, Jamie and I began to see Matsi's role as peacekeeper and as a protector of Lakota, the omega. At first it seemed that Matsi was part of the pack jostling for meat and abusing Lakota in the process. When we viewed the film in slow motion, however, we could see that Matsi was actually forcibly inserting his body between Lakota and his aggressors. He was in effect "body checking" the other wolves out of the way, offering Lakota temporary protection and the opportunity to scramble for cover.

We have not only seen this evidence with our own eyes but also heard similar scientific accounts of wild packs throughout North America. A biologist in Alaska told me of a wolf skull he had found that bore evidence of a broken jaw that had subsequently healed. A wolf with a broken jaw cannot bite, chew, or tear meat from a carcass, so how did this wolf survive? The biologist's only conclusion is that its pack cared for it until its jaw healed, regurgitating semidigested food for it, as they would do for a pup. Another report in Canada tells of a wolf pack that lost a member at

the hands of a poacher. The biologist who was tracking them reported that the pack moved in a figure-eight pattern for several days, howling frequently. His explanation is that they were searching in vain for their lost pack mate.

These scientific reports always stop short of attributing higher emotions to animal behavior. Given my experience with the Sawtooth Pack, however, I find it impossible to support the view that human beings hold a monopoly on elevated feelings such as empathy and compassion. In particular, this is the gift Matsi gave me, and it is also the most important message I can share about living with wolves.

THE MORNING GREETING RITUAL

As the first morning light withdraws the veil of darkness from the forest, the frosted grass beginning to steam in the morning sun, the wolves are still asleep. Common sense might suggest that the pack would huddle for warmth at night, but instead, they sleep a number of yards from one another, not touching at all. As if on cue, the pack begins to stir as one, without any outside physical contact stimulating the process—no elbows in the ribs, no alarm clocks. It is that same telepathic link that they seem to possess during the hunt, as though there were some central connecting thread running through the consciousness of the pack.

∽

JIM: After Jamie and I moved our camp inside the enclosure, we began to take new pleasure in the dawn, when the wolves woke up. By integrating ourselves more into their environment, we became a less-distracting presence. This ultimately allowed us to witness an even greater range and depth of wolf behavior. The very first day, we saw something we had never witnessed before—a ritual performed every morning without fail.

Motomo, first to his feet on this particular morning, pads softly over to the leader, Kamots. Assuming a subordinate position to the still-reclining Kamots, Motomo places his head entirely on the ground, whimpering softly and licking Kamots' face. The rest of the pack rises, and all of them first acknowledge Kamots in the same manner and then greet each other in turn. There is quiet but constant vocalization: whimpers and whines and, occasionally, a short, quick growl. The ritual repeats itself every morning, and the leadership and cohesion of the pack is reaffirmed.

∽

JAMIE: Jim and I were astonished when we were also included in this morning greeting. The rush of fur and warm tongues licking our faces suggested to us with much pleasure that we had been embraced and accepted by the pack. This was something they would do only once a day, whenever we first descended from the yurt platform down to their level.

We make observations—careful not to anthropomorphize, trivialize, presume, or be carried away by conjecture. In the end, however, our observations are influenced by our own humanity. ▷

BODY LANGUAGE: HIERARCHY

A whimper and gentle lick to the face indicate concern and compassion, reassurance, or respect. Conversely, the baring of teeth and accompanying growls are threatening and cautionary. The continual demonstrations of status serve to strengthen the bonds, secure peace, and reassure each wolf that it belongs to the pack.

Every gesture from the alpha signals dominance. Head and tail are held high, ears are up and alert, and the gait is smooth and confident. Interestingly, the alpha male is usually the only wolf to urinate with his leg up.

Subordinate wolves strive to keep their heads and bodies lower than the alpha's. The omega continually supplicates, with tail between legs, ears back, and every physical gesture portraying diminishment—in size and in stature.

Among the expressions of dominance and submission are also gestures of affection and kindness. Although Kamots always displayed dominance over his brother Lakota, he also showed affection by licking his face. As Lakota accepted and submitted to Kamots as the leader, Kamots reassured Lakota that he was a valued member of the pack.

ANCIENT SONG: HOWLS AND VOCALIZATION

Howling, the most legendary wolf sound, is quite complex. Contrary to popular mythology, a full moon is not the main trigger for a wolf to commence howling. Wolves may howl before feeding or hunting or emit welcoming howls when a pack member returns. Howling can announce a fresh kill or help locate a wolf separated from the group. Wolves also howl to rally the pack in a kind of celebration of unity or to respond to outside challenges. Intense sessions of play or a faraway sound may initiate howling. Howling within a territorial boundary marked by the pack's scent appears to inhibit intruders. Alone or with its pack, in daylight or darkness, a wolf will howl for more reasons than we'll ever know.

∾

JAMIE: *Winter nights became my favorite time to record the wolves. As the howl of a wolf pierces the darkness, the cold stillness seems to amplify the sound. I would set up the recording deck in my sleeping bag and run the cables and microphone outside the tent. A howl was a thrilling rush that always jolted us out of sleep. From the warm comfort of my bed, I would hit the "record" button and listen on my headphones as their songs filled the night. The beauty of their voices takes hold of you, as strong as a physical force.*

The whines, snarls, whimpers, and growls that comprise wolf communication are used to establish and maintain rank within the pack. When together, wolves almost continuously communicate with one another with low, faint whines. A higher-pitched, longer-lasting whine is used in greeting or when a wolf wants something it cannot obtain. Whining is also used by submissive pack members, partnered with corresponding body posture—lowering the body and tucking the tail—that denotes this subordinate social status. Barking indicates that a wolf is confused, agitated, or distressed. Growls accompany threats or challenges.

Wolves also communicate with sounds beyond the range of human hearing. Scientific research supports that howling and other wolf vocalizations carry individual bits of information that may distinguish each wolf with the aid of a spectrograph, or voiceprint. Over the years, as Jamie meticulously recorded the range of wolf vocalizations from each member of the Sawtooth Pack, her gift for discerning nuances in sound enabled her to identify each wolf by its voice alone. In the future, could this be a way to distinguish one wild wolf from another, eliminating the need to overmanipulate reintroduced wolves by anesthetizing and tagging them?

Vocal communication is complemented by body language—a lick to the face and mouth or a display of fangs. Changes in posture and fine distinctions in facial gestures may be obvious or slight, detectable only to the wolves or to people who have lived intimately with wolves.

Pups usually begin to howl between two and four weeks of age. They throw their heads back and adopt the posture of their elders, becoming more proficient and confident as they mature. Young or old, from alpha to omega,

all wolves participate in the complex songs and vocalizations that serve to communicate and reinforce the community structure.

∽

JAMIE: I sat with Kamots as he howled and was mesmerized by the mysterious quality of the sound. The howl of a wolf appears to resonate from everywhere, almost as if it is without source. Without conscious intention, I reached to gently touch his throat with my fingers. Kamots allowed this, throwing back his head to the heavens as I felt the vibration race up my arm. I closed my eyes and felt the ancient song surge through my body and into the earth.

intelligence, cooperation, and telepathy

Wolves are extremely social, resourceful, and intelligent animals. Their complex, integrated system of caregiving, hunting, and social bonding is considered second only to that of humans and other primates. On one occasion, the two mid-ranking wolves, Motomo and Amani, appeared to set their usual competition aside and execute a scheme for their mutual benefit. This became the subject of spirited debate among those who witnessed it.

Wolves eat intermittently, depending on the availability of prey. A young deer killed on the roadway created an unexpected "bonus" meal for the wolves, but the small portion, obviously not enough to feed all the interested parties, heightened the competition. Only the alpha and beta males, Kamots and Matsi, and the pups Wahots and Wyakin got their fill. Lakota watched hungrily but did not move from a safe position on the sidelines.

Motomo and Amani were anxiously snatching up any small scraps unintentionally cast their way. Frustrated whines were exchanged as the small deer was nearly consumed. Finally, only two disembodied hind legs and a portion of the torso remained, and Kamots seemed intent on finishing them off. As the two mid-ranking wolves approached Kamots, he issued a warning growl. They whined back, seemingly begging for food.

What followed next occurred with both precision and incredible speed. Motomo rushed directly at the carcass and seized a small piece of fur-covered meat that was lying off to the side. Kamots "took the bait" and chased Motomo, leaving the carcass unguarded. In the next split second, Amani took advantage of the opportunity, rushing in and stealing one of the remaining deer legs. Seeing his mistake, Kamots turned, but he wasn't fast enough; Amani headed for the protection of the willows with the deer leg, with Kamots on his tail. Instead of safely continuing to eat his small morsel, Motomo dropped the "decoy" and returned swiftly to grab the other hind leg, then veered off in the opposite direction. This final maneuver bewildered Kamots so completely that he broke off his pursuit of Amani and returned to stand guard over what little was left of the carcass. ▷

JIM: *Perhaps what we witnessed was a circumstance in which the wolves were merely exploiting the turmoil during feeding. However, the perfect timing and skillful execution seemed to suggest that it was more than mere coincidence and opportunism. Had the wolves hatched a scheme and then skillfully executed it?*

Perhaps Motomo and Amani had worked together. A wolf's deep-seated cooperative nature is perhaps its utmost survival skill. Wolves may lack the power and stealth of a solitary hunter like the cougar, but they have one great advantage: an evolved reliance on each other.

unexplained behavior

During their years of living with wolves, the Dutchers observed and recorded nearly every type of wolf behavior. Most was easily categorized—dominance and submission, play, mating, and so forth. However, some behavior simply defied explanation.

RAVENS AND WOLVES

Native legends from indigenous cultures around the globe and over the centuries speak of the symbiotic relationship between ravens and wolves. Ravens are to the ornithological world what wolves are to mammals: the best example within their respective classes of intelligence, complexity of vocalization, and evidence of a strong and highly developed social structure. Scientists have also observed and reported on the special, intriguing, and sometimes inexplicable relationship between these two species.

At a cool, observational level, the symbiosis may at first appear to be about the mechanics of the food chain and the business of survival. Ravens in flight spot carrion and announce the find with their piercing cries. Wolves arrive to skillfully tear up and consume the tough carcass, leaving digestible small pieces of meat in their wake for the ravens to feast upon. Or the wolves may howl to announce a hunt and ravens follow, increasing their likelihood of being first on the scene of the kill, once again to be rewarded by leftover bits of meat to consume.

What is more difficult to explain is the playful relationship between the ravens and the wolves. Scientists often define play among wild species as the acting out and perfecting of survival techniques. But some so-called play behavior appears to have little "practical skill development"—only the challenging and joyful act of play itself.

☙

JAMIE: *On one occasion, a raven landed a few feet from Amani, who was leisurely napping. The ravens were terrified of Jim and me—and try as we might, we never were able to get close enough to photograph them to our satisfaction. It was therefore astonishing to see this large, sleek, black bird prancing back and forth just a few feet*

from Amani's nose. Unable to get the wolf's attention, the raven began a piercing, raucous taunt. Amani pretended to ignore the raven, but he imperceptibly tensed his muscles and, within seconds, lunged out in the direction of the bird. Amani snapped at the tips of the raven's feathers as the bird quickly took flight and then landed a safe distance away. Amani settled down again, and the raven again came closer, strutting and crying out. Again, the wolf pounced with teeth snapping as the raven narrowly escaped. The raven continued to flirt with disaster. I watched this comical game played over and over for a full twenty minutes, each session ending in the narrow escape of the raven. Amani finally tired of the game and trotted off, ignoring the repeated cries from the raven to come back and play some more.

Any presentation of freshly killed meat always resulted in the pack's full attention given to investigating the catch, and then they'd completely devour it. When a wolf catches small prey such as a squirrel or a small bird, it might play with the prey for a while, but it will always eventually consume the animal completely. I was surprised on one occasion to find a freshly killed raven, with telltale teeth punctures. Uncharacteristically, the wolves had not made a meal out of the raven.

I picked up the bird and tossed it to the wolves. The wolves quietly regarded the inert bird as it landed on the ground. There was no response, until finally Matsi approached and gently picked up the raven between his teeth. He carried it a few yards away from the pack and gently placed the raven on the ground, then turned away from the site. His behavior indicated a sort of reverence that he never would have displayed toward a squirrel or mouse. It was as if the wolf was acknowledging that a game had gotten a little too rough and the raven's death had been an unfortunate accident.

132

A SCENE IN THE MEADOW

In July, wildflowers carpet the meadow with splashes of almost luminous color. The wolves nuzzled the grassy vegetation and appeared to pause and actually sniff the wide variety of flowers. Wolves have a highly developed sense of smell, so at first this does not seem too unusual. However, the repetition of the behavior over the course of the next few days generated wonder: What could the attraction be? Are they finding small rodents in the grass to eat?

∾

JIM: At a distance, I watch the wolves through binoculars so I don't disturb or influence their puzzling behavior. I'm astounded to see that the wolves are actually eating the flowers!

On closer inspection, Jamie further determines that the wolves are eating only one flower in particular—the shooting star. Bright, delicate magenta petals flare backward from the black stamen rimmed in gold atop the nodding stem of this wildflower. Native Americans used the flowers and bulbs of this perennial herb in their diet. When Jamie later tasted the flowers, she detected very little flavor, nothing particularly interesting or stimulating. Yet the entire pack of wolves repeated this behavior season after season, eating shooting stars, and only shooting stars, with absolute discrimination.

134

Misunderstandings
and Conflicts

wolves and dogs

For some dog lovers, there is considerable allure in the idea of living with or trying to train a wild, exotic creature such as a wolf. The body language and the behavior seem so familiar: the wagging tail, the alert ears.

However, critical differences outnumber those superficial similarities. Within each animal, dangerous conflicts war between the learned behavior that distinguishes the pet dog and the millions of years of wild nature that is the heritage of the wolf. Trying to keep a wolf for a pet or interbreeding wolves and dogs has only one outcome: trouble. The consequences can range from mere property damage to loss of life, for the wolf or even for a human being.

SIMILARITIES AND IMPORTANT DIFFERENCES

Dogs have been bred and domesticated for thousands of years to respond to discipline and training, to serve and protect human beings. Conversely, a wolf is a wild animal and won't respond when called, perform commands on cue, or be housebroken. Like other inappropriate "trophy pets" such as tigers, wolves are unpredictable, maturing from cute babies into predators that challenge their owners for dominance.

If a wolf decides to tear the furnishings in a house to pieces out of curiosity or boredom, it will. Trying to instill dog obedience training in a wolf can lead to unexpected consequences. Genetically, the wolf expects to challenge other pack members for its place in a constant daily enforcement of social standing. Wolves are extremely territorial, competitive, protective of those they bond with, and aggressive about defending food.

Even if a pet wolf appears well behaved and has never shown signs of aggression, its genetic heritage and hunting instinct can emerge at any time. An innocent child falling, crying, and struggling to get up can trigger "prey response," leading the wolf to instinctually attack and kill. The wolf is not acting deranged; it is simply following ancient instincts.

Once socialized and made dependent on humans, a wolf can never be released into the wild. It won't know how to behave or feed itself as a wild wolf

would and will frequently gravitate toward trash dumps and the easy prey of domestic livestock. Most likely, it will die of starvation, unable to hunt as part of a pack, or have its life ended by a bullet.

WOLF-DOG HYBRIDS

Wolves are an endangered species; it is illegal to traffic in or own wolves. Bred to get around the legal restrictions on owning a wolf, animals sold as "wolf-dog hybrids" are a dangerous form of genetic roulette. Interbreeding of wolves with domestic pets—often with dogs that are bred to fight—dilutes the gene pool in frightening ways, introducing unpredictability in hybrids. Dogs don't fear people and wolves stalk prey. Which trait will win the DNA battle for control?

Wolf-dog hybrids account for numerous instances of injuring people and killing livestock. If the culprit is not identified, the blame falls on wild wolves, which then pay the price for human folly, while stories about the so-called savagery of wolves are reinforced.

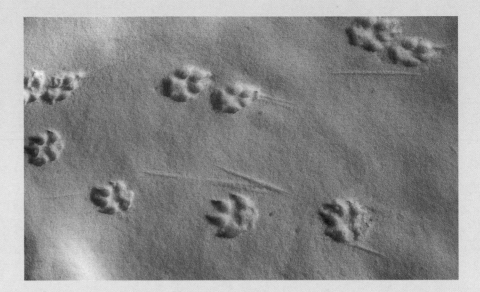

∞

JAMIE: *Jim and I regularly receive alarming phone calls from people trying to keep wolf-dogs as pets. The rescue shelters we might recommend are already filled to capacity with the tragic consequences of these misguided endeavors. The only solution breaks our hearts: the animal should be euthanized. This may sound cruel and extreme, but there is really no other humane solution. Above all, the animal cannot be set free. That "pet wolf" will harm a person or property, end up starving or being killed, or, worse, potentially corrupt the gene pool of wild wolves by mating with a wild wolf.*

Ironically, owners of hybrids or "pet" wolves are often great fans of wolves. Their respect should be channeled into supporting and protecting wild wolves, not into trying to subdue wild animals as family pets, a cruel travesty that only leads to disaster for the wolf. Most of these "pets" end their days chained in a yard, becoming mean and frustrated victims of a misguided genetic experiment, unable enjoy the social structure of the pack that is their natural heritage.

wolves of myth and legend

Throughout European history, the wolf was a symbol of darkness and evil. Incidents were reported that helped support the idea of the wolf as an instrument of the devil. During periods of war and epidemic in early European history, packs of wolves dug up the shallow graves of plague victims and were seen eating human corpses.

Veneration of the wolf had a place in Norse culture as well as in cult ritual during the late Roman Empire. Unfortunately, these groups were at odds with the growing and ultimately prevailing Christian culture in Europe. In the battle between good and evil, the wolf became a victim of religious symbolism. For centuries, this darker image of wolves was the only version revealed in mythology, fables, and literature.

HOW AND WHY MISUNDERSTANDINGS ARE PERPETUATED

When Europeans began to settle North America, they brought these well-established misconceptions of wolves with them to the new and untamed land. The colonists began raising livestock—pigs, cattle, and sheep. Wolves, being intelligent and opportunistic, did indeed pose a threat to domestic livestock. In addition, as these early settlers moved west, they severely depleted populations of game animals, especially bison, that were important prey for wolves. With little alternative, wolves turned to the sheep and cattle that had replaced their natural prey. Some historians suggest that feral dogs played a much greater role in predation than wild wolves did, but wolves never failed to take the full brunt of the blame—and the consequences.

To protect livestock, ranchers and government agencies began a campaign to eradicate wolves, and a bounty was placed on wolves' heads. Programs initiated in the nineteenth century continued as late as 1965, offering a $20 to $50 bounty per wolf killed. Wolves were trapped, hunted and shot from planes and snowmobiles, dug from their dens, and chased down with dogs. Expert wolf hunters made a living off these bounties. In addition to shooting wolves, they also used complicated snares and poison. Animal carcasses laced with strychnine were left out for wolves, also killing eagles, ravens, foxes, coyotes, bears, and other animals in the process. State veterinarians introduced canine

diseases, such as mange, into wolf communities. Even at a time when wolf populations were dwindling, the war against them escalated.

The passage of the Endangered Species Act, first drafted in 1967 and strengthened in 1973, was the first step toward a change in our national attitude toward wolves. Driven to the brink of extinction, wolves had been exterminated from the Lower 48, except for a few hundred that inhabited the far corner of northeastern Minnesota.

Wolf recovery programs continue to raise very polarizing, controversial, and emotional issues reviving the long legacy of fear and misunderstanding based on centuries of inaccurate information.

∞

JIM: *The wolves that now live in the Lower 48 are a far cry from their ancestors that once ruled the forests and plains. They are a blend of reintroduced wolves from Canada combined with the few surviving members of the original population cunning enough to avoid death by guns, traps, and poison. Today's wolves are elusive and fearful of humans, well aware that they are in constant danger. It is nearly impossible to see a wolf in the wild, and this inhibition makes it hard for humans to learn more about them. What we know continues to be a mixture of fact and mythology.*

Believing them vicious, North Americans have killed almost two million of them—and yet, wolves living in the wild have killed none of us. People understand that wolves are predators, but many still do not know the gentle side of wolves. These people never saw wolves' intelligence and compassion—with all adults sharing in watching, teaching, and caring for their pups.

American Indians, on the other hand, have had a deep respect for the wolf and for the spirit of the wolf. They have viewed wolves not as enemies but as teachers. These people sought to emulate wolves: the alertness on a hunt, their courage as they rode to battle—strong as individuals, but fiercely loyal to the other members of the tribe.

Identifying Solutions

education

❦

JIM: Our ultimate vision has been to educate people about wolves, to change attitudes and shatter the misconceptions and myths of them as evil, bloodthirsty enemies of humans. I want to achieve this goal in a nonpartisan, nonconfrontational way—and avoid contributing to the already emotional political firestorm surrounding these issues.

❦

JAMIE: Where does this story end? I hope that the results of our work linger in the hearts of people—in their minds, their emotions, and their imaginations. We want people to develop a personal connection with these animals and to see that they are, in many ways, like ourselves. Our ultimate goal is to save the wolves. But we can't save them until we can inspire people to care about them. Without this, the animal doesn't stand a chance.

But the challenge doesn't stop there. The wolf cannot be separated from the land. Any action to save the wolf must also save the habitat in which the wolf dwells. To save a species and to have nowhere for it to live other than a zoo is saving only the idea of the animal, taking it out of its natural context and placing it in a "box." In saving only the actual embodiment of the animal, you lose the emotional part, the soulful part—everything that makes a living creature uniquely what it is.

The possibility of the extinction of the wolf is a sad and depressing thought. Yet perhaps in the wolf's extinction, in a disaster of that magnitude, human beings may come to realize the grave error of their ways. Perhaps the disappearance of the wolf might pave the way for us to show another animal species a little more courtesy. If this happens to the wolf, however, we will be reduced to looking at photographs, films, and stuffed specimens. Over time, people might be curious, but they will forget. I don't hear of many people dwelling on the extinction of the Tasmanian wolf, the quagga, or the dodo bird.

In order for someone to care, that person must be able to look into the creature's eyes. From there, the animal gets under your skin and into your heart and mind. From there comes the desire to understand that animal's place on this earth with us and the desire to take the actions to save it and to save the land it needs to survive— wild and free.

wolf reintroduction

What is man without the beasts? If all the beasts were gone, men would die from a great loneliness of spirit. For whatever happens to the beasts, soon happens to man. All things are connected.

—Chief Seattle

Protected by the Endangered Species Act, wolves have begun to repopulate the most remote and wild territories, farthest from human populations and livestock conflicts. The gray wolf was once one of the most widely distributed land mammals in North America—ranging across the continent from the central plateau of Mexico to the lower Arctic region, from the Atlantic coast to the Pacific coast. Today, wolf populations in the continental United States have been reduced to only about 5 percent of their original range.

Over the last 150 years, the wolf population south of the Canadian border declined from hundreds of thousands of individuals to about a thousand—mostly in northeastern Minnesota. Brought back tenuously from the brink of extinction, a few wolves have slowly and naturally regained population in very limited numbers in small, hidden pockets of wilderness in the Lower 48, mainly in Minnesota, Idaho, Montana, Wyoming, and Washington. In addition, there are also populations of wolves in Alaska and Canada.

When wolves were reintroduced to parts of Idaho and to Yellowstone National Park in 1995, there was debate about the potential threats to elk populations and concern about impacts to the overall health of the ecosystem. Ten years later, the positive results in Yellowstone exceeded all expectations. Wolf populations are increasing, and the benefits to the ecosystem have been dramatic.

For many decades, the absence of a significant predator allowed the elk populations to inhabit virtually any area in Yellowstone that suited them. They transitioned from feeding in the relative protection of the dense forests to congregating and browsing in river valleys where food sources were easy and plentiful. This led to ravaging young trees, small shrubs, and ground cover. After the wolves returned, elk were forced to move back into the relative protection of the trees and onto the slopes where they could watch out for wolves. No

longer able to graze at will, they have had to work a bit harder to find food, with profound results.

Willows and aspen trees, instead of being eaten or trampled, now had a reasonable chance for survival and rebounded along river valleys. The recovered vegetation halted the erosion of the soil into the streams. Additional shade cooled the water temperature, resulting in more suitable habitat for trout. Migratory birds returned and found food and shelter in the recovered growth. The new vegetation provided building materials and food for beavers, with new dams resulting in wetlands and marshes that attracted ducks and other birds.

Contrary to initial fears, the wolves did not adversely impact the elk populations. Since wolves will almost always hunt game that is least risky to bring down, the old and sick elk were the first choice. Until the top predator returned, old and ailing elk cows had been able to continue breeding, an aberration that actually had a limiting effect on their gene pool. Ultimately, the wolf's return led to greater health and vitality within the elk herds. When we admire the beauty and grace of a deer or elk, we should remember that, in part, we have the wolf to thank. After ten years of scientific observation, it is now clear that the wolf is a "keystone species"—playing a critical role in keeping ecosystems healthy through natural checks and balances.

the importance of saving wild places

The Yellowstone wolf reintroduction program is a positive story. Sadly, other reintroduction projects undertaken in less-protected areas and employing different techniques have had mixed and even catastrophic results. Introducing wolves too close to developed areas usually causes conflicts with livestock interests, leading to extermination of the wolves and perpetuation of their unwarranted negative image. These programs fail to take into account the natural requirements of a wolf pack.

∞

JAMIE: *The time we spent living with wolves offered an intensely personal perspective into their family life and social nature. After seeing how they cooperate and care for one another, I am troubled by the amount of manipulation that many of the reintroduction efforts seem to require.*

Although I have tremendous regard for the biologists who are trying to bring back these endangered animals, these same scientists are caught in the center of one of the most contentious environmental issues in North America today. Good intentions often end up backfiring. Trapping, sedating, ear tagging, caging, and splitting up wolf families to haul them to unknown new territory is unnecessarily cruel and traumatic. Sometimes their new homes are situated too close to human populations. If wolves kill livestock—even on public lands—they are often destroyed to placate angry ranchers. The hatred of wolves is still so strong that many wolves end up being needlessly exterminated.

∞

JIM: *Could we not take our cues from watching what is already unfolding naturally? Allowing wolves to return on their own to wild territory far from human populations, as they have already begun to do, seems a more sustainable long-term solution. We can then work to protect them with all the power of the Endangered Species Act and work to focus our efforts on changing people's attitudes by communicating the true story of wolf society.*

Ultimately, there is only one thing that will save the wolf, and that is preserving wild spaces so that, along with other animals, they can live as an integrated whole. ▷

Even if we manage to reshape our attitude toward the wolf, it is all for naught if our attitude toward wilderness does not change. The remaining hard questions seem to end at two places: How much wilderness is enough? And are we human beings willing to accommodate this need for wild land at the expense of perceived progress?

This leaves us with the responsibility of finding ways and means to protect wild wolves by preserving the connected corridors of wilderness that they need to survive. If we continue to view nature purely in economic terms—as lumber to be harvested, oil to be drilled, land to be grazed—there will be little hope for the wilderness that remains.

Let us hope that we may yet begin to accept that nature's true value lies beyond the sum of its parts and that the mere existence of wilderness is as necessary to our humanity as it is to the wolf's survival. Only then will the wolf's precarious return to the wild be complete, and only then will future generations be able to appreciate these intelligent, complex, and deeply social creatures—and experience the delight of living on this planet, together, with wolves.

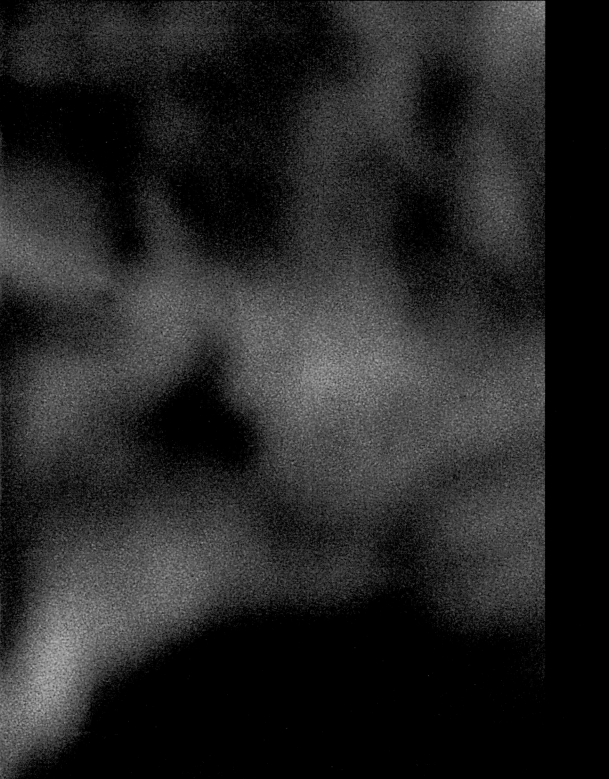

Life Size Wolf Gallery

As you turn the following pages, listen to the voices of the Sawtooth Pack

on the compact disk at the back of this book.

The scale of your hand is at a life-size ratio with the wolf images.

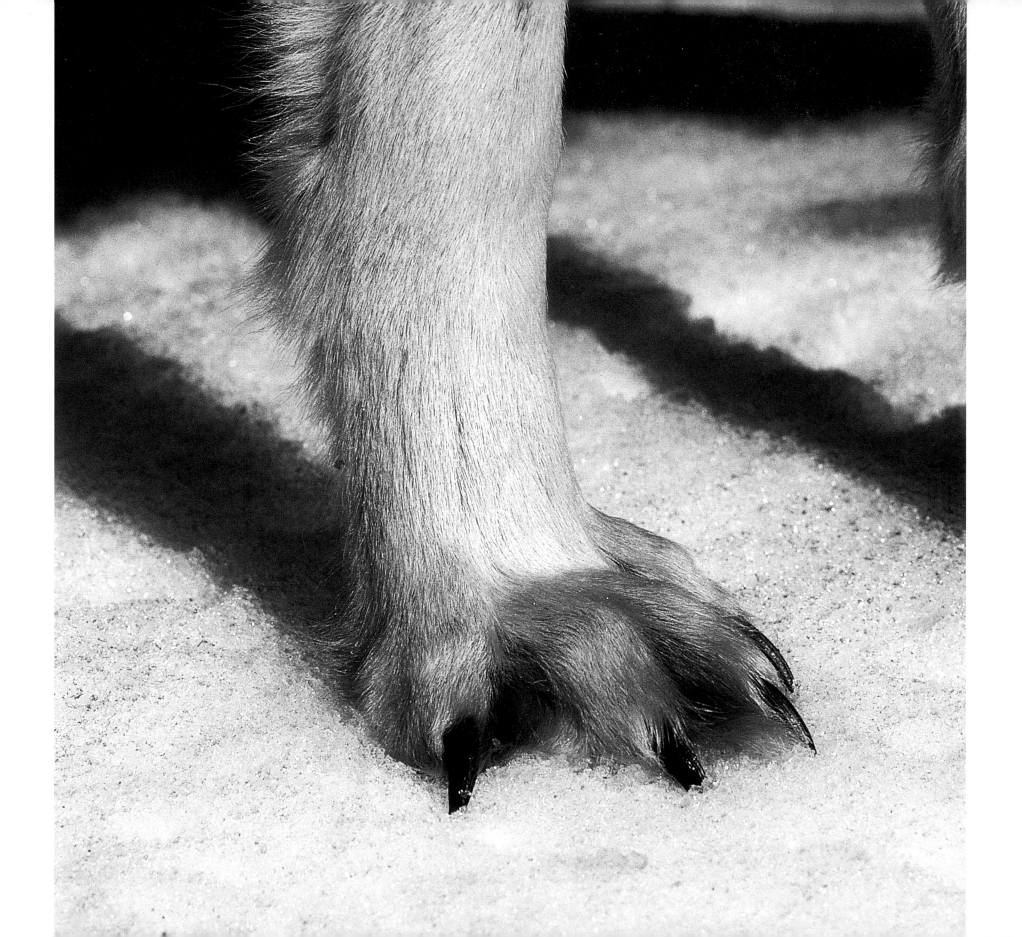

SELECTED REFERENCES

Bekoff, Mark, and Jane Goodall. *Minding Animals: Awareness, Emotions, and Heart.* Oxford, England: Oxford University Press, 2002.

Bomford, Liz. *The Complete Wolf.* London: Boxtree Limited, 1993.

Busch, Robert. *The Wolf Almanac.* New York: Lyons and Burford, 1998.

Crisler, Lois. *Arctic Wild.* New York: Curtis Publishing Company, 1956.

Dutcher, Jim, with Richard Ballantine. *The Sawtooth Wolves.* Bearsville, New York: Rufus Publications, Inc., 1996.

Dutcher, Jim and Jamie Dutcher, with James Manfull. *Wolves at Our Door: The Extraordinary Story of the Couple Who Lived With Wolves.* New York: Simon and Schuster, 2002.

Goodall, Jane, and Marc Bekoff. *The Ten Trusts: What We Must Do to Care for the Animals We Love.* San Francisco: HarperCollins, 2002.

Knight, Elizabeth, ed. *Wolves of the High Arctic.* Stillwater, Minn.: Voyageur Press, 1992.

Landau, Diana, ed. *Wolf, Spirit of the Wild.* New York: Sterling Publishing Company, Inc., 1998.

Lawrence, R. D. *The Trail of the Wolf.* Toronto: Rodale Press, 1993.

Lopez, Barry Holstun. *Of Wolves and Men.* New York: Charles Scribner's Sons, 1978.

Lorenz, Konrad. *On Aggression.* New York: Bantam Books, 1967.

McIntyre, Rick. *A Society of Wolves: National Parks and the Battle over the Wolf.* Stillwater, Minn.: Voyager Press, 1993.

———. *The War Against the Wolf.* Stillwater, Minn.: Voyager Press, 1995.

Mech, L. David. *The Wolf.* Stillwater, Minn.: University of Minnesota Press, 1970.

———. *The Way of the Wolf.* Stillwater, Minn.: Voyageur Press, 1991 .

Murie, Adolph. *The Wolves of Mount McKinley.* Seattle: University of Washington Press, 1985.

Savage, Candace. *Wolves.* San Francisco: Sierra Club Books, 1988.

Steinhart, Peter. *The Company of Wolves.* New York: Alfred A. Knopf, 1995.

U.S. Fish and Wildlife Service. "Gray Wolf: Canis Lupis." U.S. Fish and Wildlife Service, *www.fws.gov,* July 1998.

DOCUMENTARY FILMS BY DUTCHER FILM PRODUCTIONS

Water, Birth, the Planet Earth. PBS/National Geographic, 1985.

A Rocky Mountain Beaver Pond. National Geographic Special, 1987.

Cougar: Ghost of the Rockies. ABC World of Discovery, 1990.

Wolf: Return of a Legend. ABC World of Discovery, 1993.

Wolves at Our Door. Discovery Channel, 1997.

Living with Wolves. Discovery Channel, 2005.

INDEX

ABOUT JIM AND JAMIE DUTCHER

Emmy Award-winning cinematographer and filmmaker JIM DUTCHER began producing documentary films in the 1960s. His early adventures with a camera were spent underwater, part of a Florida coast childhood. In 1985, *Water, Birth, the Planet Earth*, his first film, began a career spent with animals that range from the smallest tadpoles and crabs to one of the top-ranking predators on the continent: the wolf. His extraordinary camera work has led audiences into places never before filmed—inside beaver lodges, down burrows to peek at newborn wolf pups, and into alpine meadows where cougars play in sunlit streams. His work includes the National Geographic special *A Rocky Mountain Beaver Pond*, and ABC *World of Discovery's* two highest-rated films, *Cougar: Ghost of the Rockies* and *Wolf: Return of a Legend*. Jim's intense personal involvement with the details of his subjects' lives and his eye for the beauty of the natural world have placed his work in a category all its own.

JAMIE DUTCHER, Jim's wife and co-producer, made her mark on the world of film when she won an Emmy Award for sound mixing with her carefully collected sounds of the Sawtooth wolves. A former employee of the National Zoo in Washington, D.C., Jamie is also an accomplished horsewoman who rides her hunter/jumper, Documentary, in equestrian competition.

Together, Jim and Jamie created the Discovery Channel's most successful wildlife documentary, *Wolves at Our Door*, and have been interviewed on numerous television and radio programs and in print articles, in the United States and Europe. Their most recent film, *Living with Wolves*, has been released by the Discovery Channel and continues the story of the Sawtooth wolf pack that became a part of their lives.

THE DUTCHERS live in Ketchum, Idaho, in a log house at the edge of a wild pond, with ducks, flying squirrels, elk, deer, foxes, owls, coyotes, woodpeckers, pine martens, and a mischievous black bear for neighbors.

Published by The Mountaineers Books
1001 SW Klickitat Way, Suite 201, Seattle, WA 98134

First edition, 2005

Published simultaneously in Great Britain by Cordee, 3a DeMontfort Street, Leicester, England, LE1 7HD

Manufactured in China by 1010 Printing International, Ltd.

Project Editor: Kerry I. Smith
Director of Editorial and Production: Kathleen Cubley
Research: Larry Levinger
Editor: Kris Fulsaas
Proofreaders: Christine Grabowski and Dottie Martin
Indexer: Cheryl Landes
Cover design, book design, and layout: Ani Rucki

All photographs by Jim and Jamie Dutcher, except photographs of Jim and Jamie which are by Franz Camenzind, Johann Guschelbauer, Bob Poole, Jake Provonsha, and Shane Stent

Page 28: Poem "Lemuel's Blessing" © 1963 by W.S. Merwin. Reprinted with the permission of the Wylie Agency Inc.

Library of Congress Cataloging-in-Publication Data
Dutcher, James.
    Living with wolves / Jim and Jamie Dutcher.—1st ed.
        p.   cm.
    Includes bibliographical references and index.
    ISBN 1-59485-000-3 (hardcover)
    1. Wolves—Behavior—Idaho—Sawtooth Wilderness. 2. Human-animal relationships—Idaho—Sawtooth Wilderness. 3. Social behavior in animals—Idaho—Sawtooth Wilderness.
I. Dutcher, Jamie. II. Title.
    QL737.C22D879 2004
    599.773—dc22

                                     2005005566

THE MOUNTAINEERS, founded in 1906, is a nonprofit outdoor activity and conservation club with twelve thousand members, whose mission is to "explore, study, preserve, and enjoy the natural beauty of the outdoors." The club sponsors many classes and year-round activities in the Pacific Northwest, and supports environmental causes through educational activities, sponsoring legislation, and presenting programs.

THE MOUNTAINEERS BOOKS supports the Club's mission by publishing works on conservation and history, as well as travel and natural history guides, and instructional texts.

THE MOUNTAINEERS FOUNDATION is a public foundation established in 1968 to promote the study of the mountains, forests, and streams of the Pacific Northwest, and to contribute to the preservation of its natural beauty and ecological integrity. The Mountaineers Foundation gratefully welcomes financial contributions to continue and extend its vital conservation work. Because The Mountaineers Foundation is a 501(c)(3) charitable organization, contributions are tax deductible to the extent allowed by law.

Send or call for our catalog of over 500 titles:

The Mountaineers Books
1001 SW Klickitat Way, Suite 201
Seattle, WA 98134
(800) 553-4453
mbooks@mountaineersbooks.org
www.mountaineersbooks.org

Founded in 1935, THE WILDERNESS SOCIETY works to protect America's wilderness and to develop a nationwide network of wildlands through public education, scientific analysis, and advocacy. Our goal is to ensure that future generations enjoy the clean air and water, beauty, wildlife, and opportunities for recreation and spiritual renewal provided by the nation's pristine forests, rivers, deserts, and mountains.

    If you would like to help save wild land for wild wolves, you may send your tax deductible contribution to the address below. Checks should be made out to The Wilderness Society. Please write "wolf" on your check. Thank you.

THE WILDERNESS SOCIETY

The Wilderness Society
1615 M Street NW
Washington, DC, 20036
(202) 833-2300
www.wilderness.org